BY ORDER OF THE PEAKY BLINDERS

All you Need to Know about The Gangs of Birmingham and the Tv Series

RODGE BLADE

Copyright © 2021 Ridge Blade

All rights reserved.

CONTENTS

Introduction	2
CHAPTER 1: The story first of all	9
CHAPTER 2: Where it all begins	16
CHAPTER 3: difference	26
CHAPTER 4: A series unfairly ignored	37
CHAPTER 5: A lot of alcohol	44
CHAPTER 6: Ten reason why Peaky Blinders is addictive	51
CHAPTER 7: The six is the last	58
CHAPTER 8: Death and perpetual war	66
CHAPTER 9: History	73
CHAPTER 10: Cillian Murphy	87
ABOUT THE AUTHOR	110

INTRODUCTION

Peaky Blinders is a **British** television epic about the **Shelby** family and the rise of the working class in early 20th century **England**. A true classic that was not afraid to surpass itself, reaching perfection year after year. It tells the story of **Tommy**, the head of the family, an indecipherable and tormented **Cillian Murphy**, who portrays the deep anguish of a WWI veteran after losing his wife, who sacrificed herself for him. Years later, on his knees, with a cigarette in his mouth, a few minutes before dying, he says: **"There is a woman, yes, and I love her. I've come close. I've come fucking close to having everything in life "**.

For those unfamiliar with the series, the story is set in the poorest districts of **Birmingham** in the postwar period (1919), when there was a struggle for survival in the midst of the economic crisis.
The events are centered mainly in **Small Heath**, a neighborhood where the undisputed protagonists are the **Shelbys**, a family-gang descended from the gypsies, led by the mind of **Thomas Shelby** and known as "**Peaky Blinders**".

Peaky Blinders is undoubtedly one of the most captivating period dramas of recent years. The life of the **Shelby** family, its illicit businesses and the somewhat questionable principles of group leader **Thomas "Tommy" Shelby**, manage to capture the viewer and glue him to the screen at every episode and season.

Historically this gang of criminals really existed, indeed, to be honest, in **Birmingham** of the nineteenth and twentieth centuries there were many youth gangs that triggered guerrillas and riots to obtain privileges and respect from the slums. According to historian **Carl Chinn** - as in the series - the name **Peaky Blinders** derives from the practice of sewing razor blades into the visor of hats, which could then be used as weapons. Another hypothesis is that **"peakys"** was the nickname of the model of hats they wore. Their clothing was in fact iconic: caps with visors, gilets with long overcoats and handkerchiefs, similar to another contemporary

Manchester gang, the **Scuttlers**.

In reality, the first appearance of the criminal group is dated March 23, 1890, when following a quarrel with a gang of boys in a pub, the group headed by **Thomas Mucklow** violently assaults **George Eastood**, a resident of **Small Heath**.
Eastood is seriously injured in the head and will have to undergo a trepanation operation. On April 9, the local press published a letter from a reader about a "murderous assault" perpetrated by members of **Small Heath**'s "**Peaky Blinders**".

From now on, the gang's criminal activities multiply and it will be reported for all sorts of illegal activities, from public order disturbances to violent theft. The gang was known for excessive aggression and the recurring use of improvised weapons such as forks, knives or pokers.

According to the story, the most famous members were **David Taylor** (imprisoned at age 13 for possessing a gun), **Harry "Baby Face" Fowles, Ernest Haynes and Stephen McNickle**. The girlfriends of the gang members also had a distinct style of clothing: pearl necklaces, bangs, and flamboyant neckerchiefs.

The television series, directed by **Steven Knight**, is freely inspired by historical facts and events of real news. It has been broadcast since 2013 and currently consists of 5 seasons of 6 episodes each, while we await the release of the sixth for next year. It must be said that the choice of the cast was truly impeccable, characters and settings can transport you in the blink of an eye in the atmosphere of the **Great Depression**. The pain and fear of the protagonists are so raw that time stops, and the vision of the war that has just ended is suffocating for every spectator.

In addition to all-in-one men, cold-blooded killers, power struggles and dirty strategies by the male protagonists, the series also owes its success to the role of women. All of them, wives, lovers, prostitutes, descendants of noble or desperate lineages, have written their history and their revolution.
Word by word and step by step, from

behind-the-scenes weavers have become protagonists of a sudden change of show.

The whole series is the result of an extraordinary balance between plot and story and the feeling is that each character has found its perfect interpreter.

CHAPTER 1: THE STORY FIRST OF ALL

The Peaky Blinders were a small **Victorian** age gang and were best known in **Birmingham** in the 1890s.
They were famous for their elegant way of dressing. However, their crimes were not exactly comparable to those of their counterparts in the series.
Old reports read that among their gravest misdeeds is the theft of a bike and the theft in a haberdashery shop.

The connection to reality is not just about the context in which the **Shelbys** move, but the whole history of the criminal gang: the **Peaky Blinders** actually existed, they were a notorious **Birmingham gang** involved in gambling, robberies and brawls.

Creator **Steven Knight** decided to write Peaky Blinders because his father's uncles, the **Sheldons**, were bookmakers and part of the gang business.

In an interview with **History Extra**, the author revealed that the stories his father told him gave him an initial imprint to design the TV series:

"One of the stories that really made me want to write Peaky Blinders is an anecdote. which saw my father as protagonist. His father (Steven Knight's grandfather ed) gave him a message and said: 'Go and give it to your uncle' ... My father knocked on the door *and inside the room there was a table with about eight men ... dressed in impeccable way, with caps and pistols in his pockets. The table was covered in money ... Just that image - smoking, alcohol and these impeccably dressed men in this Birmingham slum - made me think that that was mythology, it is history, and it is the first image that I have started working ".*

The differences between reality and fiction

The real Peaky Blinders date back to the 1890s rather than the 1920s as the protagonists of the tv series. Most of their members were young and some could be as young as 12.

They were a street gang and didn't

have the political ambition that **Tommy** shows across the show's five seasons. However, when it comes to violence, the real gangsters have gone even further than **Tommy** and **Arthur**. In addition to robberies and skirmishes with rival gangs, they also attacked the police. According to **Steven Knight's** stories, their violence was truly ferocious.

The showrunner, quoting his uncle's words, told **The Mirror:**

"They didn't care about each other. They were like fighting dogs."

The origin of the name

Their name is said to derive from the razor blades placed in the visors of their hats. **Historian Carl Chinn** (source Birmingham Mail) has suggested that this is most likely just a myth.

Razor blades began to be used only at the end of the 19th century and therefore were economically prohibitive at the time.

It is much more likely that their name derives from the tips of their hats and the fact that "blinders" (which literally means "who blinds") was jargon for their neat looks and impeccable clothes.

The Peaky Blinders ruled the streets of Birmingham for decades but by the 1910s they had lost the power to rival the Birmingham Boys gang. Although they had lost the top spot, the term "Peaky Blinders" is said to have been taken as a terminology to refer to any street gang in Birmingham. **Billy Kimber**, the leader of the **Birmingham Boys**, may even be a role model for Tommy. A secondary character in the first season, in real life Kimber was charismatic and intelligent and became the most powerful gangster in **England**.
Kimber had another base in **London** and formed alliances with other gangs in **Leeds** and **Uttoxeter**.

THE END OF AN ERA

It wasn't just the growing domination of other bands that led to the end of the Peaky Blinders.

The police became more severe and the sentences they passed caused many to turn away from these illicit groups.

Children went to school more and more and learned discipline and the new boxing clubs offered many alternatives to joining street gangs. In the 1920s the remaining Peaky Blinders moved to the countryside and largely disappeared from sight while the **Sabines** (the **Italians** featured on the show), a rival gang of the **Italian mafia**, claimed all their Birmingham territories.

CHAPTER 2: WHERE IT ALL BEGINS

With an unsurpassed script, **Steven Knight** navigates double-breasted bandits, clandestine betting and horse racing, describes the ambition and discord between family members and the power of corrupt politicians and authorities - something akin to what we are experiencing in this, of a century.

All of them choke on their own greed as they make their way through the streets to survive or to take control. On the surface it is a series about mafia and gangs, but in reality it is about the class struggle in the 1920s and about a man who dreams of leaving crime behind to lead an honest life. However, there is no room for misunderstandings. To overcome adversity, Tommy Shelby must bring out the worst in himself and deal with his calculating and murderous instincts, which will lead him to an eternal battle with his demons.

It is a mistake to think that Peaky Blinders is a series about **British** culture. The story takes place between tormented men who have experienced the atrocities of war and shows the impact this has on social and family relationships. It is also a reflection on their way of dealing with the mistakes of a dark and convulsive past, and on their optimistic outlook on the future, as well as on the way they care for their loved ones. "That kind of experience: finding yourself in a difficult situation with your family, surrounded by others in the same conditions. In fact we hear about many people who 'live well': I don't know where you come from and how you grew up, but in the real world there are too many who live like the characters in the series, or like me and my father "assures **Caryn** referring to his father, a second-rate Chicago gangster. "He wasn't exactly a mobster, and I'm sure he didn't want to enter that world. He bet a lot, he was sad. He was the kind of person who could be in debt to characters like **Tommy Shelby** ".

Steven Knight hails from the same place where Peaky Blinders takes place. His parents grew up in **Birmingham** in the 1920s. His mother ran a clandestine betting business. In those days it was illegal to gamble on horse racing and children were used to raise money. At the age of eight he had started walking the streets with a basket full of clothes and the bettors left an envelope with the money and the number of the chosen horse. His father as a child was a delivery boy for his uncles, the **Sheldons** (the BBC asked for their surname to be changed), bookies known as 'Peaky Blinders'. "He told me that he had knocked on the door and they had opened it, there was the smell of cigars and whiskey. Once inside, he had seen a round table covered with money, in a place where no one had any, a place where people were hungry and walked around barefoot. He said the men seated at that table were impeccably dressed, with polished weapons, knives and shoes. They drank whiskey and beer in jam jars because they didn't spend money on glasses. Those people only cared about how others saw them, they only thought about money ".

Throughout his childhood, **Steven** listened to the stories and memories of his uncles and grandparents. He grew up playing in the same places where part of that story took place. "Pubs are small and dirty. It's not a nice environment, but it's magical, and with Peaky Blinders I wanted to turn it into a myth, just like they do in the **United States** with cowboy movies. " Many times he skipped school and wandered around scrap yards with his father, a gypsy who made horseshoes for work, one of the traditions of his paternal family. "There were horses and very interesting people. There were gypsies, second-hand dealers. It was the bottom rung of the **Birmingham** working class. Peaky Blinders is about this. Of all that I have come to know and experience of that world ".

Knight decided to tell a daily story in which misfortune and misfortune abound. From his point of view, there is not much room in the drama for ordinary people with normal lives, where everything goes well. "The role of drama must be to explore what happens when things go wrong. This is the road that leads to the darkest places ".
Knight is well aware that the role of the playwright is to offer the audience

characters they can identify with. It then exposes individuals, who are also relatives, to difficult situations, and shows us how they behave in the worst circumstances.

Birmingham is not a well known city in the **UK**, it never has been. So the idea of writing a series about 1920s mobsters set here was a real personal challenge for Knight. Failure was by no means excluded.
"It was about taking the risk of being inspired by our context and fixing the streets in which I grew up in an image. In any place it can be found in a great story".

One of the most appreciated features of Peaky Blinders is undoubtedly the historical-aesthetic refinement of its settings which have become iconic over the years. We have seen the first events all around **Small Heath**, an area basically made up of factories and modest homes, located in the **South-East** area of **London** and linked to it by a river, the **Gran Union Canal**. But where was this series shot and built?

Obviously over time the aforementioned area has transformed, abandoning the features of the historical period affected by the events of Peaky Blinders, so those who worked on everything have alternated places taken from some cities such as **Manchester, Yorkshire, Liverpool**, applying to them the appropriate patchwork.

The main street where we see the debut of the Shelby family, for example, whose name is **Watery Lane**, really existed, except that it was destroyed during the postwar period, leading the series to rebuild everything in **Powis Street**, a street of **Liverpool**.

An important location for the filming of Peaky Blinders is the **Black Country Living Museum** in **Dudley**, a museum linked to the birth of the **Industrial Revolution**.
This offered a lot of elements related to the construction of iconic places in the plot.

Another iconic place is the Grand mansion that Tommy buys in the third season.

Its name is **Arley Hall** and it is located in **Cheshire**, it has belonged to the **Ashbrook** family for 500 years and has now become a tourist venue for events and filming.

The **Garrison** is also one of those places that has remained in the hearts of fans of the series, pub and the heart of some of the strongest developments. Unfortunately for the fans its existence is to be found among the sets built specifically for the plot. There is a **Garrison** to **Small Heat** but it has nothing to do with the series.

CHAPTER 3: DIFFERENCE

Maybe they didn't always say "by order of the Peaky Blinders", but they really existed: that's what happened to the real **Shelbys.**

There are many fans who have become passionate about the history of the infamous Peaky Blinders and who for several years have been following with bated breath all the cunning tricks of Thomas Shelby. But who, finding himself in front of one of his henchmen in real life, would smile hearing him utter the now iconic phrase: **"by order of the Peaky Blinders"**.
Yes, because, as we have already said, the protagonists of Steven Knight's

drama really existed, and while luckily they didn't manage to enter politics, they did many of the things reported in the series. Let's find out who they were, what happened to them and how their story got on television.

There was no distinction of sex, age or gender when the Peaky Blinders came into action. Among their crimes, robberies and assaults were the order of the day, as were extortion and smuggling, and almost always the dead came out.

The real Tommy Shelby

Thomas Shelby and his family, unfortunately or fortunately, didn't really exist. However, the character played by **Cillian Murphy** follows what is now remembered as the greatest organized crime boss in Britain: the leader of the **Birmingham Boys, Billy Kimber**.

Born in 1882 in Birmingham, **Kimber** was a charismatic and very cunning man. When the gaming law was instituted in 1845 that banned all recreational activities except racing, Kimber formed an alliance with the **Hoxton Gang** to take over all the racecourses in southern **England**. Thanks to alliances with other gangs in Leeds and Uttoxeter and with the mafia boss **Charles 'Wag' McDonald**, Kimber also took total control of all races in South London, the Midlands and North UK. His life ended in 1942 when he died after a long illness at **Mount Stuart Nursing**

Home in **Torquay**.

And to think that in the series **Kimber** appears as a minor character. And instead…

The real Alfred 'Alfie' Solomons Jr.

Yes, the character played by **Tom Hardy** really existed! As reported by **The Jewish Chronicle**, in the early 20th century a **Jewish** gangster named **Alfie Solomon** (the s was added in the series) allied with the Italian mobster **Darby Sabini** (which we will discuss shortly) to take control of the illegal trading in north **London**. Together with his brother **Harry**, **Solomon** ensured that **Jewish** bookmakers were protected, creating a climate of respect and terror.

In 1921, **Solomon** also tried to kill

Billy Kimber in front of **Sabini's** apartment, but was acquitted because strangely all the witnesses "lost their memory".

In a letter he wrote in 1930 and retrieved from **J-Grit: The Internet Index of Tough Jews**, it was discovered that at one point he even proposed himself as a police informant in exchange for protection from a group of men they had threatened. to kill him. "Since I was released from prison, I have begun to live a respectable life, keeping my bets and staying out of trouble," he wrote. His dominance ended when a rival Birmingham gang (the **aforementioned Boys**) staged a shooting in **Bath** during a race, which went down in history just like the **Battle of the Baths**. Harry was arrested for threatening to shoot a policeman. Nothing has been reported of him since the early 1930s.

Who was Darby Sabini?

The gangster **Darby Sabini** instead came from an **Anglo-Italian** family in **Little Italy**, in **Clerkenwell**, before becoming the most feared gangster in southern **England**.
In the police records of those years, his name was reported several times, especially during shootings during racing. Over the years he managed to keep control of local betting, winning over the rival gang of the **Cortesi** brothers and the **Hoxton** clan. But his power was based on an alliance between **Italian** and **Jewish** bookmakers, so with the advent of

fascism and the progressive spread of **anti-Semitism**, his whole kingdom collapsed in one fell swoop.

After being arrested and jailed for three years, during which time his only son was killed in **Egypt**, **Sabini** moved to **Hove, Sussex**, where he ended his days working as a bookmaker.

Oswald Mosley

The character played by **Sam Claflin** also really existed.

The English politician **Oswald Mosley** was born in 1869 in **Mayfair**, into a wealthy family.

After attending **Winchester College**, he enlisted as a cadet at the **Royal Military Academy at Sandhurst**.

When World War I broke out, he

volunteered to join the air force; but while he was bragging about what he had learned, he seriously injured his ankle and was dismissed. At the end of the **First World War**, at the age of only 21 he began his political ascent, being elected as a deputy for **Harrow** and passing within a few months from the conservative party to that of the separatists, to then join the **Labor party** and try to defeat **Neville Chamberlain**, without success.

The rise and founding of the British Union of Fascists

In the series we see him a few years later, when, after leaving the **Labor party**, he decided to found the **British Union of Fascists**, an extremely anti-communist, protectionist and isolationist party, which aspired to become the English version of the **Mussolini** dictatorship.

Among his biggest supporters was **Lord Rothermere**, the owner of **Associated Newspapers Ltd**, who printed the **Daily Mirror and the Daily Mail**, and who in 1933 had the front page "hurray for the black shirts!" His enthusiasm, like that of so many other party supporters, waned a year later when 12,000 fascists violently beat their opponents and the **British Union of Fascists** also began to follow anti-Semitic lines. However, in the early days of World War II, party membership increased again, under the false promise of peace in exchange for support for the **Nazis**. In 1940, the **British Union of Fascists** was banned from the government and **Mosley** was incarcerated at **Holloway Prison**, along with his wife, **Diana Guinness**, nee **Mitford**, one of the famous six Mitford sisters who became celebrities in those years for their different political views - she was very attached to the figure of **Hitler**. Subsequently, he tried to get back on the crest of the wave, but eventually had to surrender to his defeat and move to **France**, where he died in 1980. In addition to him, many will know by name his son, **Max Mosley**, the former president of the **Fédération Internationale de l'Automobile (FIA)**.

Aside from the fact that most of the characters didn't really exist, as **Chinn** always explains in his book, the most important difference between the **Shelbys** and their historical counterparts is the era.

In the series, the gang operates between the 1920s and 1930s, while the real Peaky Blinders started acting undisturbed as early as the 1890s. **Billy Kimber**, by the way - the real **Thomas Shelby** - deserted the war, so she has never suffered from **PTSD**. Politics has never been of interest to him and his actions, in reality, have been even more violent than you have seen in the series: in addition to robbing and fighting against rival gangs, he and his men have attacked the police several times.

CHAPTER 4: A SERIES UNFAIRLY IGNORED

The **British** media network **BBC** is the main promoter of innovative and original television formats and subjects, and many of their serials have achieved global fame, proposing themselves as an excellent alternative to the most famous **American** names. For example, series like **Sherlock** and **Doctor Who** are now institutions in the sector: the former exceeds 20 million viewers worldwide and the latter has become the face of **British** science fiction for more than 50 years. But the **BBC** brand is also found in smaller but equally deserving productions, often ignored by many viewers. This is the case with Peaky

Blinders.

Entirely written and produced by **Steven Knight** (known for the particular movie Locke), the series tells the criminal rise of the Peaky Blinders, a street gang that really existed between the 19th and 20th centuries, whose name derives from their cruel practice of blindness through a razor blade hidden in the hat.

Leading the group is the Shelby family, whose middle brother Thomas (**Cillian Murphy**) holds the role of gang leader. The story starts in 1919 in **Birmingham**, with the physical and psychological scars of the **Great War** still fresh in society.

The gang runs an illegal racecourse betting round, but during a theft they accidentally find a load of heavy weapons belonging to the **British Crown** and decide to use it as a bargaining chip for future political alliances. They will soon enter the sights of the **IRA** and the **British government** itself, and in particular the cunning **Inspector Campbell (Sam Neill)**.

An interesting premise and of excellent depth, which seems to be inspired by the beautiful **Sons of Anarchy** from which, however, it clearly differs for the issues dealt with, linked to the particular and fascinating historical period.
In the dirty industrial districts of **England** you can breathe the air of social revenge of the veterans, abandoned by their country: there are those who embrace the communist

ideology and call for illegal strikes in the factories and those, like Tommy, take advantage of this moment of transition for easy earnings and to rebuild a new identity. The anti-hero is disillusioned and tried by the senselessness of the conflict, and at night he is haunted by the ghosts of the German shovels digging into the walls. We make his acquaintance when he feels the emotional detachment from the family and struggles to trust others, but at the same time he is committed in every way to guarantee a future for his brothers.

Cillian Murphy is an English actor who in recent years has participated in numerous productions (28 days later, **Sunshine** and **Batman Begins**) and in this show he plays a role with which he shows all his acting skills. The new patriarch of the Shelby family is shrewd and cautious, with a unique charisma with which he manages to make even a highly decorated police inspector uncomfortable. Once, however, in the intimacy of his room, the protagonist reveals all the fears aroused by the war and the consequent addiction to the opium he uses to find sleep. A multifaceted character who dominates the scene and alone pulls the strings that move the rest of the family and also of many opponents.

The villain of our Tommy is a very good **Sam Neill** (whom many remember for the role of the paleontologist in **Jurassic Park**), who in the role of the man of law shows the friction between those who want to do their duty and those who use the police means for their own purposes. His hatred of the Peaky Blinders transforms him drastically, shatters his honor as an old-fashioned gentleman and makes him meaner and more vengeful than the criminals he fights.

The winning element of the show, which differentiates it from other productions, is undoubtedly the aesthetics: similar to what is seen in the films of director **Guy Ritchie**, the industrial and **post-Victorian** world of Peaky Blinders appears even more dirty and battered than what it actually was, thanks to the accurate and impactful scenography, and to the desaturated colours that create lively visual contrasts with the glimpses of the **English** countryside. The numerous action scenes are punctuated by a music as dark and angular as the characters, and it does not matter if the soundtrack is not aligned with the historical period and leans towards alternative rock or even punk, because each song integrates perfectly. in the situation. The result is a product that is not only visually and scenically impressive, but also fun to follow thanks to an ever-pressing pace.

Despite its innate qualities, very little is heard of the show among fans. Could it be due to the fact that it appeared on BBC Two in the motherland and was poorly distributed internationally?

CHAPTER 5: A LOT OF ALCOHOL

Why does Peaky Blinders generate so much appeal to the general public? How can a story about criminals, about subversiveness, about violence, gather so much audience?

It is not such a strange phenomenon, given the success they have had, TV series like **Gomorra** and **Suburra**. The dark side of society can generate a magnetic effect, partly for almost **Freudian** reasons, attracted by the forbidden and the taboo, partly because they are often stories that create the last, the disappointed, in search of redemption against power on stage. preconceived, come precisely in the case of Peaky Blinders.

The Peaky Blinders are in fact war veterans, an atrocious war, decided by others, others who have not entered the battlefield. What they witnessed in the trenches is something unimaginable, capable of changing anyone. Here we find part of Thomas Shelby's charisma: a man ready to make his way at any cost, looking for a redemption from that life that has already killed him in his soul. And the moral, what will it be? All that remains is to wait for the next seasons and the finale to find out.

"The noble experiment" was defined as prohibition, a term that indicates the prohibition of the production, sale and consumption of alcohol in America between 1922 and 1933.

The proponents of this prohibition had been fundamentalist and moralist groups of both a political and religious nature and the provision was sanctioned by the **Vostead Act** of 1929, which entered into force on January 16, 1920. This provision, which had the objective of reducing the crime and illegality rate, had exactly the opposite effect: on the evening of January 15, 1920, the crowds went to refuel the last bottles sold legally and also attacked the vehicles that transported alcohol. This ban increased the prestige and wealth of the criminal society, which worked to sell alcohol on the black market and at very high prices. On Tuesday, December 5, 1933, thirteen years after its entry into force, the end of the validity of the **Vostead Act** was sanctioned and millions of Americans were able to start buying alcohol again legally.

Among the numerous topics covered in the TV series Peaky Blinders, in the fourth season the one that emerges most is that of alcohol exports to **Ireland** and **America**. If initially the Shelby family's business was concentrated on illegal bets on horse racing, over time, that is, when thanks to Thomas' dangerous strategies the family manages to get rich, the attention shifts to the production and sale of alcohol smuggling.

But how was it possible to get large quantities of alcohol to America? The allies on the territory were certainly of substantial importance, but this was not enough, so what to add?

A hedging activity, of course! Thomas agrees to transport the spirits inside the crates containing objects of his legal activity, namely the manufacture of car parts. Inside the crates with the spare parts inside, the crates of alcohol were also inserted which, in this way, reached their destination without being discovered. The combination of several families made everything possible, but we should not underestimate the importance of the collaboration of the forces of the order who often closed both eyes by letting the smuggled goods pass.

WHISKEY

As in most of the series, the Peaky Blinders series is also linked to whiskey and, above all, its indelible protagonist, Thomas Shelby.

Whiskey is a proof method: it tells you who is authentic and who is not.

Old Bushmills Irish whiskey has imposed itself as a paradigm of Tommy's morality from the very beginning - as merciless as it is capable of loving without limits.

Intelligent and brave, the ice-eyed boy carries the weight of the entire family on his shoulders, taking them from the struggle for survival to a prominent place in **Birmingham** crime.

Willing to kill and sacrifice so much in order to maintain his leadership, Tommy often takes refuge in a reassuring glass of **Old Bushmills**. On the label that appears during the episodes, the whiskey bears the ancient name which over time has changed into the current **Bushmills** 10 Years Old.

A whiskey, a rum and a gin have been dedicated to Peaky Blinders, so much has been the impact that the series has had on the audience of passionate drinkers.

The **Old Bushmills Distillery**, located in the far north of Ireland, is the oldest whiskey distillery in the world. This began its activity in 1608, when Sir **Thomas Phillipps** was granted a license by **King James I** to be able to distill.

CHAPTER 6: TEN REASON WHY PEAKY BLINDERS IS ADDICTIVE

There are many reasons why it is addictive in the series, too few to mark in a single book.
For this, I have tried to summarize the 10 that are most important to me.

1. There is no scene where they don't drink whiskey and don't smoke cigarettes. If he's not already sucking it in, Tommy Shelby takes it out of the package; if you thought you were healthy with this TV series you will change your mind because the cigarette ritual becomes magnetic and an hypnotic gesture.
It is the cigarette that characterizes the

machismo of the protagonist, together with a glass of **Scotch** whiskey taken in the **Garrison Pub**, the family's place where they meet in the private room. Tommy in the series expresses himself on the use of different spirits:

"Rum is for leisure and for sex, isn't it? Now whiskey, there is business!"

2. If you meet him, your only thought will be having sex with him. Thomas Shelby's character has the irresistible charm of the villain, calculation and coldness in business, a tender heart with women. With them he reveals the gentle, sensitive and romantic side; the women smell and try with all their weapons to seduce him or take a ride. But Tommy, of a suspicious and hermetic nature, will lose his head for

only one of them, **Grace**, whom he will marry and to whom he will dedicate a very touching letter, once lost:

"Life is a suffering that must be lived in silence, dirtying an old ink sheet, away from prying eyes. We cannot show ourselves weak. I can't, I don't have to. You managed to shatter the walls of my steadfastness, my determination and my strength. For this I hate myself. I hate myself Grace, but I have always loved you, this is the greatest truth. "

3. Female characters are awesome! They are intelligent, enterprising women, they are the ones who manage the moods of their companions.
Linda, the puritan **Catholic** moralist

wife of **Arthur**, far from her husband's wicked life, will abandon him, throwing him into despair. **Michael**, the power-hungry son of **Polly**, will find in his **American wife Gina** the perfect partner capable of playing with cunning and cold blood. **Aunt Polly** will be the staple of the family, she will have a maternal side that the **Shelby** boys lack, and the male hand of those who hold the power and administrative management of the company.

4. Impossible to forget just one of the characters in the story, anyone who comes into contact with the Peaky Blinders will acquire character and personality, each leader of the enemy bands, each passing woman who will try to take the place of their beloved

Grace.

Bizarre and bewitching the role of **Grand Duchess Tatiana Petrovna**, a rich **Russian** princess dressed in diamonds and precious stones, who would sell her mother for money and for a free life marked by orgies and caviar.

His is the sentence addressed to Tommy Shelby: "I put in 500 pounds more for sex".

5. Explicit violence will creep under your skin like blood in your veins; gun duels are transformed into an artistic moment, foul language will enter your lexicon so much that it will be difficult to respond to a message without starting it with a "fucking bastard".

6. At the end of the first season your

only thought will be to find a racecourse and a good amount of money to spend on a horse named "**Grace**".

7. The change of look will become a lifestyle: remove every jeans from the wardrobe, you will make room for a double-breasted coat in worsted wool, long black or anthracite gray coat, strictly tailored tweed suits, shirt with club collar, wool vest from which check out an elegant pocket watch, tie clip and the legendary flat cap inside which you will sew a razor blade ready to be thrown as a weapon.

8. You will never go near a church anymore. Arthur's wife Linda is such a fanatically religious character that you hate all sorts of believers. His

momentary conversion to the Shelby's nefarious life will be hardly credible. Nights that are good at smoking, drinking and throwing cocaine will not take off that puritanical veil of an exalted **Catholic Christian**.

In fact, he will soon return to pray and invoke the name of God, but we had already imagined it.

9. If your job does not satisfy you, you will think about the political career.

Thomas Shelby in the fifth season became a **Labor MP** elected by popular vote.

He will try to "clean up" and lead a respectable life. But don't forget that before the party, he went through shady deals!

CHAPTER 7: THE SIX IS THE LAST

"I found him, the man I can't beat."
We left Tommy Shelby (**Cillian Murphy**) in despair as he screams in the fog, with his wife's ghost behind him, pointing a gun to his head.

He, the absolute protagonist of the "Peaky Blinders" series, has perhaps for the first time found who is truly able to hinder his rise from the squalid underground betting house in the slums of post-WWI Birmingham to the top of British politics.

Adventures reconstructed with great accuracy of detail, in costumes and sets, punctuated by a soundtrack of great impact, ranging from **Nick Cave** (his is the song of the theme "Red Right Hand"), **Iggy Pop, PJ Harvey and Jack White**.

Warning: spoilers

The head of the infamous Shelby family, called Peaky Blinders perhaps for the "pointed" visors of their caps lowered over the eyes or for the custom of sewing razor blades into the cuffs of hats, over the span of 5 seasons he measured himself with the secret services of the Queen and with the Russian tsarists who escaped the communist revolution. He escaped the revenge of the ruthless **Luca Changretta (Adrian Brody)**, exponent of the bloody **Italian mafia** (at the time **Black Hand**) in **New York** and got the better of a very hard confrontation with the gang led by

Alfie Solomons (**Tom Hardy**), crazy and intelligent Jewish preacher.

He saved his family from the gallows when the hangman's noose was already tightening around their necks, signing an iron pact with none other than **Winston Churchill**. An agreement that allows him to transform a near-defeat into a victory and acts as a springboard for his political career. But now he risks losing the comparison with what he himself defines "the devil", or **Oswald Mosley** (**Sam Claflin**), founder of the **British Union of Fascists**, a real person who had close contacts with **Mussolini** and **Hitler**, almost a **Mephistopheles** incarnation of the spirit of her time.

One of the peculiarities of the

successful **BBC** series, visible in **Italy** on **Netflix**, is in fact that of skilfully mixing historical facts and characters (Oswald Mosley is also the father of Max Mosley, president of the International Car Federation from 1993 to 2009) , with elements of fantasy: the Peaky Blinders and Thomas Shelby really existed, even if their story began around 1890: they were a Birmingham gang involved in gambling, robberies and fights.

They were noted for their elegant style and violent ways. The creator of the series, **Steven Knight** decided to write the script because his father's uncles, the Sheldons, were bookmakers and were part of the gang business.

"One of the stories that really made

me want to write Peaky Blinders - said Knight - is about an anecdote about my father. His father (Steven's grandfather ed) gave him a message and said: 'Go and give it to your uncle' ... My father knocked on the door and inside the room there was a table with about eight men ... flawless, with caps and pistols in his pockets. The table was covered in money ... Just that image - smoking, alcohol and these impeccably dressed men in this Birmingham slum - made me think that that was mythology, it is history, and it is the first image that I have started working ".

But this we just said..

The **BBC** confirmed the last season by announcing that it would resume production in the UK under strict **Covid** guidelines.

And the first turn of the handle was given on Tuesday 19 January, with a delay of just under a year compared to forecasts.

The sixth season is also written by **Steven Knight**, **Anthony Byrne** will remain as director after the previous season.

Filming began on Tuesday, January 19, 2021, with a delay of just under a year compared to forecasts. Hopefully the new episodes will arrive by the end of the year, but it all depends on how quickly the production can complete filming in the midst of the virus crisis that is plaguing the UK.

"Peaky is back and with a bang - said Knight - After the forced production delay due to the pandemic, we find the family in extreme danger and the stakes have never been higher. We believe this will be the best series of all. and we're sure our amazing fans will love it. " Then the screenwriter made an announcement that aroused further curiosity: "As the TV series draws to a close, the story will continue in another form."

Steven Knight, aroused the curiosity of fans of the series with this announcement.
Then, with an interview with **"Deadline"** he clearly explained what the future of his show will be: *"Covid has changed our plans. However, I can say that my idea was, from the very beginning, to end 'Peaky Blinders' with a film. This is exactly what will happen "*.

As Thomas Shelby would say:

"When everyone backs away, it's time to move forward."

CHAPTER 8: DEATH AND PERPETUAL WAR

"Every morning and every evening we should continually think about death, feeling already dead for ever, in this way, we will be free to move in any situation."

Thus reads the eighth assumption of **Hagakure,** one of the fundamental books of samurai ethics written by **Yamamoto Tsunetomo.**
What does an eighteenth-century book have to do with a contemporary TV series?

As we all know Thomas Shelby is a young veteran of the **First World War,** like his two brothers.
Over the course of the very short

seasons, the **Birmingham** family, thanks to Tommy's brilliant instinct, manages to forcefully climb the social hierarchy to the point of gravitating around the figure of **Winston Churchill**.

It is precisely Thomas' qualities that make the difference: he seems to draw strength from the war that has strongly traumatized him, the use of drugs and the copious consumption of alcohol and cigarettes testify, at the same time, the inner weaknesses of this character. However, unlike his older brother **Arthur**, Tommy almost always lets himself go in moments of exclusive personal reflection, coldness and firmness during decisive or critical negotiations, as well as in the organization of highly sophisticated strategies.

Several times during the four series, Thomas claims that he is already dead. His enemies address him as the man who is not afraid of dying: Tommy died in **France**, while digging the tunnels to save as many soldiers as possible;

The Tommy gangster, on the other hand, lives after defeating death because he is no longer afraid of it, having already known it on the front.

Here we connect to **Hagakure**. From the point of view of superiority over death, Thomas Shelby represents in all respects the warrior "free to move in any situation". It may seem absurd to connect a character from a **British Netflix** series to the complex samurai world.

Yet Tommy perfectly embodies the individual who has managed to free himself from the oppressive chains of the fear of death: he has definitively eliminated that limiting ego to which the entire work of **Tsunetomo** refers ("feeling already dead forever").

The theme of liberation from the fear of dying is dealt with several times and in an accurate way throughout the series.

Polly, Thomas's aunt and second in chief given her enormous charismatic and political qualities, in the last season claims to feel stronger, safer and freer, after escaping a certain hanging for just under a second. Following a brief period of drug addiction and depression, **Polly** will return to lead the family alongside

Thomas, eliminating the weaker side of her temper that had caused some problems for the **Shelbys**.

In Thomas's case, the theme of death must necessarily be placed side by side with that of perpetual war. The profound trauma of the **Great War** indissolubly binds the young leader to a dimension of continuous inner war.

So Thomas feels at ease only experiencing the conflict, perpetually reflecting on how to defeat the opponent or protect himself from the enemy. There is no peace or serenity: life makes sense in war.

Here, too, we can connect to the great names of the land of the **Rising Sun**. In "spiritual lessons for young samurai", **Yukio Mishima** argues that the total lack of war has softened the post World War II Western bloc, of which **Japan** is also a part: war is necessary for the realization of the individual.

The connection between Thomas Shelby and Japanese culture must clearly be taken with due distances: Tommy is still a negative figure, a veteran strongly resentful of the institutions and the strong powers that allowed the cruelty of the Great War to take place, a disenchanted ex-Marxist, a bloodthirsty and devilishly Machiavellian leader.

The parallel with the land of the samurai occurs only and exclusively for the reason thanks to which Thomas always succeeds in the realization of his objectives: defeat death, annihilate fears and weaknesses of our ego that conditions us, often negatively, we can live free.

It is up to us to decide for what purposes and for what causes.

CHAPTER 9: HISTORY

Let's start with the historical reality. In 1890 the Peaky Blinders are a criminal gang made up mostly of violent and troublemakers.

They are mostly kids from **Small Heath**, a neighborhood blackened by the fumes of the factories, watered down and muddy, poor and overpopulated, a miserable and dilapidated slum where the law does not reach and therefore the beatings and aggression are the only solution.

They do not have a razor hidden in their hat with which they deliver lethal blows, as in those days a razor blade was a luxury that not everyone could afford, but they resort to frequent use of improvised weapons such as pokers, forks and knives.

With the arrest of some, if not many, of the members, the Peaky Blinders disappear as they were born.

At the beginning of the twentieth century the band of the **Brummagem Boys** appeared: the stone on which **Billy Kimber** later founded the **Birmingham Gang** in the 1920s.

Started as a gang of pickpockets, the **Birmingham Gang** extends control and power to **London** horse racing, clashing with **Charles "Derby" Sabini,** an **Italian** mobster and undisputed master of the tracks making **Billy Kimber** one of the most feared gangsters in the world.

The television series

Twenties of the twentieth century, Thomas Shelby is the man behind the growing expansion of the Peaky Blinders who, from the muddy streets of **Birmingham**, rise to conquer the power of the city first by snatching it from **Billy Kimber** and then, over the seasons, they face **Charles Sabini** stealing from him the crown of **King of the Racing**, they ally with the **Jews of Alfie** (an impressive and majestic **Tom Hardy**), work secretly for the fallen **Russian** nobility and suffer heavy losses from the **Italian-American** revenge of **Luca Changretta** (an incomprehensible and speckish **Adrien Brody** who collects everything that an Italian emigrant to the **States** could do in the 1920s including an artichoke hand and toothpick in his mouth) to finally arrive in the polling booths of **Birmingham**.

The Peaky Blinders, or rather, Thomas Shelby does business with everyone: from gypsy racing makeup artist and horse lover to secret employee of **Winston Churchill**, from astute overseas bootlegger to indispensable politician and respectable businessman and, in the of four seasons, the razor blade hidden in the hat becomes a revolver and then a vote on a ballot paper, all with great expenditure of blood, tears and suffering.

Fiction therefore goes beyond reality and reality lets itself be carried away by fiction towards a collective imagination, pulp and pop, which is enriched with new characters and new caricatures.

It matters little (see **Vittorini,** 2017) that the real Peaky Blinders were only violent kids and that, probably, the creator of the series **Steven Knight** had drawn more inspiration from the events of **Billy Kimber** (later transformed into the obstacle to break down of the first season), what interests us is the cognitive stimulus it brings with it: **Birmingham**, the years between the two **Great Wars,** the veterans of the First and the nascent socialist movements, **American Prohibition** and the promised land for **European** distillers, the growth of a family and the elevation of man to **Emperor.**

All these factors and all these elements stimulate the imagination and break up and reassemble to create something new and something known, something already seen but still unknown, something familiar but always foreign and alienating: the gangster.

Reality is less interesting than fiction, especially when it comes to this sometimes mythical figure. It can also be said that there are low intensity myths and they are those myths in which no one thinks they have faith, but which bounce from one text to another creating a network of cultural and media references, for example vampires or zombies. , the western or, precisely, the gangsters.

They are mythologies that have no absolute value, they are not God or Religion, but they are cultural creators created to respond to cultural and psychological requests that bounce between different media once under film, another under comic, yet another as song or book or oral story.

The gangster condenses on himself a strong dose of violence and eroticism, combining the mythology of the young dead star with that of freedom, of the self-made man and the modern difficult man, of **Mary Shelley's Prometheus**.

However, if his deeds may seem like a revenge on the oppressing society, in reality there is no doubt that his work is evil, negative, profligate, made up of alcohol, drugs, prostitution, murders, robberies and violence, just think of names like **Jimmy Diamond, Johnny Torrio, Al Capone**, men gone down in history as great gangsters and men of evil.

Is it right then to raise such abject and criminal characters to "myths"?

What happens if murderers and robbers are idolized? Are these really the myths you want to talk about?

It is useless to remember useless and empty debates on the responsibilities of television series, on **Gomorrah** and on attempts at emulation, the evil is in the eye of the beholder, even vampires and zombies are meek, but this does not mean that people suck blood or eat brains. (or at least not all). The myths we want to talk about are those that strike the collective imagination, those that win in entertainment clashes.

In a culture and in a society that esteem and venerate the winner (in which society is this not done?) The gangster always manages to collect respect and fascination, both when he wins and when he loses everything. Often the gang star is greedy, clever and disgusting but it is in the fiction that reality becomes captivating.

"This place is under new management ... by order of Peaky Blinders"

Thomas Shelby from the first season is no ordinary thief or swindler, he is the heir to a dynasty of men who spit in the face of their fate and fight to get what they deserve: dignity and respect. And he does it with gun in hand, with bullets and gunpowder as he prepares to climb the heights of the hierarchy.

Thomas Shelby and the Peaky Blinders are not afraid to get their hands dirty with mud, grease and blood to continue their social ascent, they struggle to get away from their criminal, ruthless and greedy origins, they buy villas in the hills or in the posh neighborhoods of Birmingham, they dress as businessmen, but nevertheless, despite everything, they remain inextricably linked to their roots.

Leaving the muddy streets of **Birmingham**, leaving that evil place of **Small Heath** is the primary and driving reason for everything, however when danger looms and there you take refuge: where it all started, where it all began.

In his essay **Pupe**, cars and guns, **John Gabre** highlights the fact that the city is a chimera of concrete and asphalt to be tamed: "it serves as a background to the gangster and is the symbol of the desolation that produced it, as well as the extension of its own brutality."(Gabre, 1976).

The gangster, Thomas Shelby, is an integral part of the city of Birmingham, he takes the side of the defenseless, of the mothers without husbands, of the poor people.

He protects his family, his gang, his city. The gangster Shelby is father-master, he is paladin and ogre, he is the protector and pimp of his city.

Everything must change, so that nothing changes

Weapons, power, old ladies, gangs, cars, alcohol, gangsters are all the same whether they are **California** bikers or **British** pub thugs, they represent that mythopoeic charm that television series feeds on and that captivates viewers: the bad guys.

The bad boys are the backbone of drama, they are the hundreds of words spent in nonfiction books by television critics, they are the reason for subscribing to **Netflix**, **Amazon Prime** or **Sky**, they are the pepper on the porridge of contemporary television, they are the hook for a successful series.

Thomas Shelby, Jax Teller, Walter Heisenberg White are the allure of evil, sadistic and sick mythology that raises reprehensible characters and attitudes to popular icons, mythology that the viewer is able to endure and appreciate because it is limited to stories in which we can already read the epitaph, in which the characters enter already loaded with their tragic destiny on their shoulders, because after all we know that the end of the gangster is to die "dead killed". And if for Thomas Shelby and the Peaky "Fuxxking" Blinders the destiny has not yet been written and will only be discovered in the next season, for all the others it is not a spoiler to say that, in the end, at least in fairy tales, the bad guys always lose.

Violence, alcohol and smoking in abundance that almost make the liver and lungs uncomfortable, incomprehensible dialects and a story that goes without saying, all elements worthy of a great television series.

CHAPTER 10: CILLIAN MURPHY

The last chapter of this book is an honor to those who made this possible: the figure that will remain indelible in our minds by Tommy Shelby.

It would have been different if it had been played by someone else instead of the fantastic **Cillian Murphy**.

Manchester, January 11. It is a winter morning, the temperature does not exceed two degrees and it is the last week of filming of the fifth season.

In an old studio completely adapted for Peaky Blinders is **Cillian Murphy**, quiet. He is not in a hurry. He is dressed as Tommy Shelby. Flawless. It has become more robust than in the first few seasons.

His seriousness on set is intimidating. Between takes he remains silent, making concentration a mandatory exercise. In the times, in the entrances and in the dialogues it is of millimeter precision. His grave voice resounds throughout the study; **Murphy** follows the director's instructions precisely. He's delivering **Tommy's** last lines in a very heated scene with the **Shelby** brothers.

His character was painstakingly constructed by **Knight**: he is an intelligent strategist, but at the same time - as the story progresses - his intelligence turns into a personal limit. He is emotionally fragile. His mind can be his worst enemy. He does not sleep well, he heals himself, drinks and uses drugs in search of some relief. And, in the midst of the misery and darkness of his emotions, not being afraid of death continues to be his main motivation.

Tommy is full of contradictions and behavioral inconsistencies, he is violent and manipulative, but also sensitive and weak.

"Human nature is like this, there are nonsense facets in everyone, there is this duality ...
This is the beauty of television: it gives you the opportunity to get to know a character for more than thirty hours. You can delve into every little detail, you can shed light on that part of his psyche that is usually not seen. He has charisma, even if people don't

necessarily want to be close to him, they are fascinated by his motivations, by the reasons why he does what he does. I believe that people identify with that determination, that relentlessness ".

Even though Tommy Shelby is a Knight creation, Murphy has completely taken possession of the character. His ability to compare vulnerability with being rude is unique. His tormented gaze reveals the confusion, the spirit of revenge, the cruelty of a criminal in search of redemption.

In the sixth episode of the fourth season we hear **Radiohead's Pyramid Song**: "I realized something. There is no peace for me in this world. Maybe in the other ", exclaims Tommy, after having emerged victorious from a bloody war with the Italian mafia under the orders of Luca Changretta, played by Adrien Brody, and at that point there is a moment of catharsis: a few hours before Tommy is elected deputy for the **Labor Party**, his deepest demons emerge.

The series has the advantage of being able to highlight the harsh and dark aspects of the disadvantaged classes and, starting with a character like Shelby, describes the rise of the working class of a society regulated on the basis of caste, based on the place where one is born. "One is not what it becomes, but how it is born, period. You can't change it, but Tommy tries, "says Murphy. The script promises the possibility of making it, but in the end it exposes the reality of the characters without euphemisms. "I've learned one thing these days: those bastards are worse than us. The politicians, ladies and gentlemen. It doesn't matter if we're entitled to it or not, they will never accept us into their buildings because we are who we are and we come from where we come from, "says Shelby.

For **Murphy**, this role means being master of your own destiny. He is used to being a favorite of some of the best film directors, such as **Christopher Nolan** and **Danny Boyle**. But his responsibility in Peaky Blinders goes beyond just playing a character. On set, Murphy is a born leader. His point of view on how to bring Knight's story to the screen is decisive. His opinion on the character, very clear. "For me this is not a gangster, but rather a man wounded by the First World War. One who experiences conflict and is full of contradictions. People feel attracted to these kinds of characters, who have a different moral code. And of course it is a very fascinating world. I think what Steven and I have accomplished is about working class people, about people who, unlike the aristocracy or the rich, originally had nothing. " To prepare this character, he moved away from the most obvious references and preferred to read up on the First World War and the post-traumatic stress that men suffer after the conflict. He assures that he was not inspired by the famous gangster sagas: "I've never seen The Sopranos. I've seen all of Scorsese's films, but they didn't help me to make Peaky Blinders ". He had long conversations with Steve Knight about the story and the character, which consolidated season after season. At this point, after five seasons, Peaky Blinders couldn't exist without **Cillian Murphy**. "Tommy is not a vain type, I think he likes to dress well, because at the time having that image of style and class, being the center of attention, was just a matter of clothing. I am quite the opposite. I don't like being the center of attention ".

Even after five years of playing Britain's most beloved contemporary gangster, Murphy doesn't have much in common with his character. "Some of his decisions are totally immoral." And she doesn't think it necessary to identify with him to play him: "You just need to understand why the character is behaving that way. Even though it looks like he's manipulating or using his family, Tommy always has good intentions in the end. This approach helps to understand it ".

Murphy is not the kind of actor who approaches parts from some personal affinity and never puts his ideology or thoughts into play. He sticks to the script to try to understand the character's emotional situation. "Steve Knight is pretty careful to avoid getting personally involved," he assures.

Cillian Murphy was born in Ireland to a family of teachers and grew up surrounded by books. His parents have always pushed him to reading and a love of music, his passion for the arts comes from there. They all went together to listen to Irish music. "In those days, nobody around me worked in the entertainment world, they were all teachers". His father was a bass player in a band and had met his mother at a concert. Cillian has been passionate about music since he was a child, he remembers having started listening to the Beatles at the age of five. "I am very proud to be Irish. Mine is a country of storytellers: it has a great artistic tradition, good writers, good actors ". Murphy began to devote himself to the arts primarily for his love of music. His musical tastes ranged from **Stevie Wonder to Pink Floyd**.

He quickly learned to play guitar and drums, then set up a group with his younger brother. After a few years, they came close to signing a contract with a record company, but they were still minors and in the end nothing came of it. It was on that occasion that they offered him his first part in a theatrical performance, and that immediately became his second passion. He went to **London** looking for opportunities and then there was the boom. "It was a very important change, it is now part of **Irish** history. The emigration of all artists in the eighties and nineties ...

It seemed essential to leave, express themselves and return. For me it was fundamental.

London was an exciting city and it was essential to find a personal voice ".

Disco Pigs was his first theatrical production, with which he toured for eighteen months. Four years later, he also became the star of the show. And, later, he found himself on the set of **28 Days Later of Danny Boyle**.

Cillian Murphy is a kind man. It is cultured. She loves listening to music and spending time walking around **Dublin** with her children. It is quite the opposite of Tommy Shelby. Totally disinterested in power and fame, he does not lose sleep with the ambition of ending up on the cover of magazines or participating in major film productions. He prefers to divide his time between independent films, theater and, in recent years, Peaky Blinders.
If he has something in common with the Shelbys' breadwinner it is that they

can both be reserved and introverted people. He is the kind of actor who turns into a mystery to public opinion. And maybe it is precisely that mystery that continues to make him an enigmatic person. "I'm old school, I think an actor should be an actor, period. I want to do things properly, the rest doesn't interest me ".

In Peaky Blinders Murphy is as seductive and sophisticated as **Johnny Depp** in **Public Enemy.**
He has the temper, calm and wisdom of **Al Pacino** in the **Godfather** and the charisma of **De Niro** in **Heat**.
With that character he went to a very dark and personal point, where anguish and thirst for power coexist. A glance is enough for him to convey

what he has in mind. His silences are eloquent. He continually tests himself and his character makes us think that all our demons are there to make us swing between pain and uncertainty, between bitterness and hope.

It shows us how to hit rock bottom, how to go to hell to understand that we never want to go back.

CONCLUSION (Review)

A TV series not for everyone but to be given a chance

As you can guess from the rest of the book, this series is one of my favorites.
Despite this, I would not call it a proposal suitable for everyone.

In all honesty, the first time I approached Peaky Blinders, it had bored me at times, not arousing much interest on my part. Now, as a fan, I can say that this is a show that conquers you little by little, that it takes time to be appreciated for what it really is. Above all it needs special attention on the part of the viewer.

I was about to leave him. Fortunately, with the famous "second chance",
I discovered a product that can leave its mark and make you really excited, able to show you the more "intimate" side of a character like **Tommy Shelby**, who survived the First World War and became the head of the Birmingham mafia, the Peaky Blinders group.

The depth of this character and the way in which his story is told piece by piece, analyzing every single inner aspect, is truly exceptional and makes the soul vibrate to the depths.

We are shown all the devastating impact of the First World War on the dismembered soul of Tommy and his brothers who, between alcohol and drugs, try to go beyond their devastation.

Tommy is already "dead" in the tunnels dug during the war, he will repeat it several times over the course of the series. He is already dead and this is a strong point for him: he is no longer terrified by the primordial fear inherent in the human being, he no longer has the fears and instincts that characterize him.

The details that leave their mark

A strong point of this TV series is given by the details: from the depth of each individual character to the careful analysis at a historical and costume level, arriving at the perfect structure of the dialogues.

The settings are unique and recreate a perfect Birmingham of the twenties in the midst of industrial development: in the midst of the first cars and the endless factories linked to the industrial development of the turn of the century.

Even the brutality and cruelty of the show are another of his strengths, his way of proposing the mafia wars without filters make it particularly characteristic.

We would hardly be able to find defects in Peaky Blinders which, especially in the advanced episodes, also manages to offer us some interesting political implications, when the relations between politics and mafia families are analyzed more closely.

In short, the reasons to see this TV series are really many: from the details taken care of with extreme attention, to the emotional situations that never fail to amaze us positively, from the individual growth and humanity of the characters to the perfect reconstruction of the places of the time.

So I invite you to try it if you have never seen it (even if I know that you are passionate like me).

Peaky Blinders is an incredible TV series, which marks the birth of a very particular and innovative genre, which shows us a different mafia from the one we were used to.

Masterful interpretations, very detailed and really well made settings and costumes, as well as a particular care of the characters, make this TV series a truly complete proposal. Super recommended!

Of course, there is still a lot to say about this fantastic story, but too little to put into one book. For this, our first trip to England in the 1920s ends here!

WAIT, I was almost forgetting, I have prepared a **FREE BONUS** content just **FOR YOU** that you have finished reading this book.

To request it is very simple, just send an email to: rodgebladeproduction@gmail.com writing **BONUS** as the subject.

Acknowledgments

This book was made possible thanks to the many people who brought me here. I try to remember them all, thanks to my roots, my teachers, my guides: my grandparents, Carl and Lucy.
Through their teachings, their thoughts, their love, through their manifestations, their culture, their inventions, through their example, their normality, the ancient and precious world that they transmitted to me, I have built my shelter. , my refuge, I have placed it deep in my heart and return to it every time I have to lick my wounds.Thanks to my parents, Judy and Joseph, who gave me life, opened my eyes to it and then

they taught me everything ... even the ability to question their teachings. Thank you also for having accompanied me, at all times, in that extraordinary discovery that is human existence.

Thanks to Simon, precious guide in the construction of the path that leads you to realize your dreams, for his availability and for his innate, immediate, generosity. Thanks to Jake Olmos for the ancient teachings that I have never forgotten and for throwing me with confidence into the world of sharks, a survivor of which I realized that I could be myself. Thanks to all those who have always been close to me and who have helped me in the writing this book.

ABOUT THE AUTHOR

My name is Rodge, I am 42 years old, and I live in Meriden. I am a writer by profession and I decided to write my book on Peaky Blinders because I am a history buff.

The fact that it was filmed right near my hometown gave me even more inspiration to write because I know first hand the reality that my countrymen lived in the past because of the underworld and I am happy to share my experience with you!

Made in the USA
Monee, IL
29 April 2021